T0196062

BOOKS BY LOIS LEWIS

The Magnanimous Gift

The
HUMMINGBIRDS
Will Return

POEMS AND PROSE POEMS

Lois Lewis

WESTBOW
PRESS®
A DIVISION OF THOMAS NELSON
& ZONDERVAN

Scriptures taken from the Holy Bible, New International Version®, NIV®. Copyright © 1973, 1978, 1984, 2011 by Biblica, Inc.™ Used by permission of Zondervan. All rights reserved worldwide. www.zondervan.com The "NIV" and "New International Version" are trademarks registered in the United States Patent and Trademark Office by Biblica, Inc.™

WestBow Press books may be ordered through booksellers or by contacting:

WestBow Press
A Division of Thomas Nelson & Zondervan
1663 Liberty Drive
Bloomington, IN 47403
www.westbowpress.com
1 (866) 928-1240

Print information available on the last page.

ISBN: 978-1-9736-0468-6 (sc)
ISBN: 978-1-9736-0470-9 (hc)
ISBN: 978-1-9736-0469-3 (e)

Library of Congress Control Number: 2017915728

WestBow Press rev. date:11/14/2017

In Loving Memory
of Onnie Lois Wigginton

CONTENTS

INTRODUCTION

Ernest Hemingway is reported to have said, "There's nothing to writing. All you do is sit down at a typewriter and open a vein." And Robert Frost wrote, "no tears in the writer, no tears in the reader."[1] I didn't comprehend the truth of those statements until I wrote my first collection of poetry, *The Magnanimous Gift*. The theme of that maiden collection was, searching for God. The main theme of this second collection is the providence, or protective care, of God. I admit, I shed a few tears writing both books.

I would feel remiss if I didn't mention, where scriptures are included in my writing they appear out of context, and may be paraphrased or incomplete. I would also remind readers, though poems often mirror a writer's unique experiences and thoughts, they are imaginary constructs.

---

[1] Preface to Collected Poems, 1939

But ask the animals, and they will teach you,
or the birds of the air, and they will tell you;
or speak to the earth, and it will teach you,
or let the fish of the sea inform you.
Which of all these does not know
that the hand of the Lord has done this?
In his hand is the life of every creature
and the breath of all mankind.
Job 12:7-10

Squirrels

In the ancient Ozark woods,
furry acrobats
high in the tops of the oaks and hickories,
sway their bushy tails side to side
balancing on tightrope limbs
as they leap, tree to tree.

And when winter winds blow cold rain,
snow and ice, I think about them
high in the crow's nest of their tree ships,
snuggle-wrapped in their long bushy blankets
like resting Iditarod sled dogs,
nose to tail.

And I know
from where God sits enthroned
above the circle of the earth,
people look like grasshoppers,[2]
and He keeps watch
over every squirrel.[3]

---

[2] Isaiah 40:22
[3] Psalm 50:10–11

Something Amazing

I bought the prettiest gift bag at a Cracker Barrel Old Country Store. Decorated with birds and flowers, it has a saying written on it, "Every Seed Grows Into Something Amazing." That brought to mind a scripture:

When you sow, you do not plant the body that will be, but just a seed, perhaps of wheat or of something else. But God gives it a body as he has determined, and to each kind of seed he gives its own body.[4]

That scripture got me to thinking about the seemingly endless variety of seeds that become flowers, trees, fruits, and vegetables; and the different tastes, smells, sizes, shapes, and colors that enrich our lives,

like the yellow kernel that becomes a green stalk, and an ear with a brown tassel, and hot buttered corn-on-the-cob; and the premium bird seed that grows into giant sunflowers that turn their faces to follow the sun, and end up next to a shed in a Van Gogh painting; the smell of pine when the wind blows through the trees, and an orange when you peel it; wildflowers coloring fields and hillsides; the taste of a ripe tomato picked fresh off the vine, and the juicy sweetness of a freestone peach; crisp celery stalks that flavor a pot of homemade soup; wheat waving in the fields before being baked into loaves of warm yeast bread slathered with butter, and plump blackberries that find a home in grandma's cobbler.

---

[4] I Corinthians 15:37-38

Red Fox

Red fox cocks his head
to the side, then back,
then to the side again –
                    listening, keenly.
It is the dead of winter
in Yellowstone. The snow is
six feet deep. Red fox listens
as if his life depends on it.
Suddenly! he springs
high in the air.
His body arcs as he
nose dives into the snow.
His rear legs and tail are
all that are sticking out.
When he pulls back
like a wine cork popped from a bottle,
a mouse is dangling
from his lips.
If I hadn't witnessed it
I wouldn't have believed,
what sensitive hearing
God gave red fox.

Flip to the Funny Pages

My parents used to subscribe to the Sunday newspaper
because mom liked to clip coupons,
and dad liked to flip to, "the funny pages."
One of my favorite memories is of him
sitting in his recliner holding the newspaper,
laughing out loud at the comic strips.
He would often tell us which ones we needed to read –
Beetle Bailey, Dennis the Menace, Blondie, Hi and Lois,
Marmaduke, Family Circus, he read them all.

Now that I think about it, that may have been
what first attracted my dad to my mother. She had a
wonderful sense of humor, and laughed easily.
They were married over sixty-four years,
and lived into their eighties.

Medical science now reports there are many health benefits
of laughter - it helps lower blood pressure, reduces anxiety
and stress hormone levels, improves cardio health by
getting your heart pumping, works your abs as your
stomach muscles expand and contract, boosts T-cells
that help your immune system fight off sickness,
triggers the release of endorphins – the body's natural
pain killers, and produces a general sense of
well-being. It's interesting to me
to note, how long it takes science
to catch up with the Bible.
Thousands of years ago Solomon wrote,
A cheerful heart is good medicine . . .[5]

5   Proverbs 17:22

Paddle and Pray

In the early eighties
I was on a whitewater expedition
in Arizona and Utah
when a thunderstorm seemed to come out of nowhere.
Twelve of us in three rafts
bobbed like corks through the rapids.
Canyon walls prevented us from
getting off the water. Lightning bolts were
striking all around,
and there was nothing to do
but paddle and pray.

Like many summer storms
it passed fairly quickly,
but at the time it felt like it lasted forever.
Thankfully everyone survived unscathed,
and I learned a great lesson that day –
when prayer is all you have,
you have everything you need.

Indigo Bunting

The beautiful melody I was listening to
through the open window
came from a tiny turquoise-blue bird.
The online Audobon Field Guide identified it
as a male indigo bunting –
a member of the cardinal family
that often migrates at night
using the stars for navigation.

In Homer's Odyssey, Calypso tells
Odysseus to keep the Bear (Ursa Major)
on his left hand side, and at the same time observe the
position of the Pleiades, the Bootes, and the Orion
as he sailed eastward from the island of Ogygia.

Can you fathom
this tiny scrap of sky
possessing the God-created equivalent
of a computer chip
encoded with celestial navigation instructions?

Before the Cradle to Beyond the Grave

I breathed into your nostrils the breath of life.[6] I engraved you on the palms of my hands.[7] I numbered the hairs of your head.[8] Your DNA is unique – your fingerprints, voice print, and iris pattern too. I knit you together, [9] gave you eyes to see the beauty of creation, ears to hear birdsong and music, a brain to store wonderful memories. Choose to follow me, and my Holy Spirit will live inside you.[10] My angel will encamp around you.[11] I will go before you and level the mountains.[12] I'll walk beside you, hold your right hand.[13] I'll be your rear guard.[14] My eyes will search throughout the earth to strengthen you.[15] I won't slumber or sleep,[16] grow tired or weary.[17] You can trust me.[18] As long as the earth endures, seedtime and harvest, summer and winter, day and night will never cease.[19] I will send rain to water the earth,[20] put a rainbow in the clouds,[21] provide you with food, water, and clothing.[22] I keep my promises.[23] Don't be afraid, [24] don't worry,[25] don't doubt.[26] Even

---

[6] Genesis 2:7
[7] Isaiah 49:16
[8] Luke 12:7
[9] Psalm 139:13
[10] I Corinthians 3:16
[11] Psalm 34:7
[12] Isaiah 45:2
[13] Isaiah 41:13
[14] Isaiah 52:12
[15] 2 Chronicles 16:9
[16] Psalm 121:4
[17] Isaiah 40:28
[18] Proverbs 3:5
[19] Genesis 8:22
[20] Ezekiel 34:26
[21] Genesis 9:13
[22] Matthew 6:25–33
[23] Joshua 21:45
[24] Isaiah 41:13–14
[25] Matthew 6:25
[26] James 1:6

to your old age and gray hair, I will sustain you.[27] I'll lead you with cords of human kindness.[28] I will always tell you the truth.[29] I am your rock,[30] your strong tower,[31] your mighty fortress.[32] I'll walk through fire for you.[33] I'll fight a giant,[34] a den of lions,[35] the devil.[36] I'll do for you, what you can't do for yourself – buy you back with my blood.[37] I'll remove your sins as far as the east is from the west,[38] sweep them away like the morning mist,[39] remember them no more.[40] I am your shepherd. If you get lost I'll search for you, and carry you close to my heart.[41] No one can snatch you out of my hand.[42] I'll prepare a place for you[43] like no eye has seen, no ear has heard, no mind has conceived.[44] Your death will be precious in my sight.[45] I will come back, and take you to be with me.[46] I'll wipe every tear from your eyes.[47] I'll sing you a song.[48] I'll give you my peace.[49] I'll make you victorious.[50] I want you to live with me forever. I love you with an everlasting love.[51] I give you my Word.[52]

[27] Isaiah 46:4

[28] Hosea 11:4

[29] Hebrews 6:18

[30] Psalm 78:35

[31] Proverbs 18:10

[32] Psalm 18:2, 46:7

[33] Daniel 3:24–25

[34] I Samuel 17:45–47

[35] Daniel 6:22

[36] I Corinthians 15:24

[37] Hebrews 9:14

[38] Psalm 103:12

[39] Isaiah 44:22

[40] Hebrews 8:12

[41] Isaiah 40:11

[42] John 10:27–30

[43] John 14:2

[44] I Corinthians 2:9

[45] Psalm 116:15

[46] John 14:3

[47] Revelation 21:4

[48] Zephaniah 3:17

[49] John 14:27

[50] I Corinthians 15:57

[51] Romans 8:38–39

[52] 2 Timothy 3:16

Starfish

I've always liked Loren Eiseley's story, "The Star Thrower,"
which has been adapted and circulated in different
versions for close to fifty years. One version tells of
an old man walking along a beach littered with starfish after a storm.
Knowing they would die out of the water, he was picking them up
one at a time, and throwing them back into the ocean. A boy who
saw him commented about how many there were, and asked
if he thought he was making any difference. The old man
picked another one up, threw it back, and said,
"it made a difference to that one."

The only sea star, or starfish, I've seen in person
was in a gift shop near the beach - dried, brittle,
and long dead - arms displaying rows of sharp bony, spines.
The internet video I watched showed a live one -
headless, brainless, regenerator of lost arms -
advancing by means of tube feet, wrapping its arms
around a clam shell, prying it slightly open,
dropping its inverted stomach into the crack
where it digested the clam. Don't you find it fascinating
the various ways God provides food
for each living creature?[53]

---

[53] Psalm 136:25

Artesian Well

In a pasture beside a rural dirt road
water has consistently flowed
from a small pipe for generations.
Its source is saturated sandstone
deep within the earth.
Even in times of severe drought
it has slaked the thirst of
man and beast.
Makes me think of the
ever flowing
streams of living water[54]
present in the hearts of believers,
freely available to tap into
day or night –
spring, summer, autumn, or winter –
the unlimited power
and guidance
of the Holy Spirit.

---

[54] John 7:38–39

Cows and People

An octogenarian in Kansas once told me
about the bull she and her husband named
Samson, "just like in the Bible." She said
they raised him from a, "baby calf,"
and he grew up and killed her husband.
Reminds me of evening news stories
about two-legged animals.

Of late I've been ruminating
about cows and people.
When we are young,
before anyone tells us we can't,
like the cow in the nursery rhyme
we believe we can do anything –
even jump over the moon.

From the mid-thirties to the nineties
when we turned on the T.V.
we might have seen Elsie the Borden cow's
smiling face encouraging us to
sweeten our dispositions
by eating Peach Blossom ice cream.

When the storms of life come our way
we head for what we think will be
safe shelter. Sometimes like the
ten cows lying dead under a giant oak
we get struck by lightning.

Other times we are blindsided
like the twenty-five thousand head of cattle
that froze to death standing up
facing into the wind in a Colorado blizzard.
Had they turned around,
the wind might not have gotten into their lungs,
and the snow probably wouldn't have
become packed in their nostrils. Hindsight is
twenty-twenty.

Now and then, cows and people
show a lot of smarts –
like the cows I saw crowded next to
the exhaust fans of a chicken house
on a smothering hot summer day.
God gave them enough sense to know,
sometimes you have to put up with the stinky
stuff in life in order to gain a greater good.

Roaring Lion

The National Geographic special,
Lions of the African Night, was graphic.
I can still hear the warthog's terrified squeals
as a lion ripped open his soft underbelly,
and devoured his intestines. In His Word
God warns us about our enemy, the devil,
who prowls around like a roaring lion
looking for someone to devour.[55]

If I allow myself to dwell on that
frightening thought, I am transported back
to nineteen seventy-five when I closed
my eyes, and stopped my ears, in a movie theater
because I couldn't bear the tension I felt
listening to the soundtrack of *Jaws* –
    knowing the shark was closing in
on the woman swimming, unaware
of his stealthy presence.

---

[55] I Peter 5:8

Duckbill Platypus

No one can convince me
God doesn't have a sense of humor.
    Native to the rivers of eastern Australia,
the duckbill platypus is a mammal – that lays eggs.
It has a bill like a duck, a tail like a
    beaver, and legs that stick out to the side
like a reptile. It also has fur like an otter,
walks on its knuckles, burrows tunnels on
    land, and hunts underwater.
Adults have no teeth, and swallow gravel
that aids in digestion. Minus a stomach,
    their esophagus connects directly to their intestine.
Prey is detected through electrical sensors
located on their bill. Males have venomous
    ankle spurs on their back legs.
Females have no nipples –
milk is produced through skin pores.
    I'm not making this up.
What a hodgepodge creature!

Spinner of Plates

Unicyclist, balloon twister, guitarist, rag-time pianist,
magician, gymnast, zip code aficionado
who can describe the place where you live –
they're all here on a four block pedestrian mall known as
Pearl Street in downtown Boulder, Colorado.
You can watch people walk on stilts, do back flips
and card tricks, juggle fire, and spin plates.
For all that is going on it is surprisingly quiet.

People meander through, watching and listening,
occasionally dropping change in hats or guitar cases.
I'm glad there are places like this where free spirits
can earn a modest living. The spinner of plates is one of my
favorites. It's a balancing act – plates on poles, keep
them all spinning. Reminds me of omnipresent God –
everywhere at once,[56] making sure what needs to
take place does, at the time that it should.

The sun rises and sets, tides come in and go out,
clouds form, rain falls, rivers flow, crops grow.
A woman giving birth screams, her baby does the same.
An old man dies. A star burns out. An angel serves a saint.[57]
A bird falls to the ground.[58] To escape a predator, a rabbit
hides beneath the same ground. A beaver fells a tree.
A doe nurses a fawn with a bobbing tail.
The blowhole on a dolphin closes as he dives.
Summer comes south of the equator, winter comes
to the north. The largest plate keeps spinning –
the earth revolves around the sun.

---

56 Jeremiah 23:23-24, Hebrews 4:13
57 Hebrews 1:14
58 Matthew 10:29

Box Turtle

Driving the curves around Mountain View, Arkansas,
one day a box turtle was in the road
as I crested a hill. There was no time to swerve –
it sounded like a gunshot,
and in the rearview
I saw the splatted turtle.
Oh, how I hated that.

Did you know a tortoise shell is composed
of sixty bones, and the varied colors
and marking patterns of the shell are unique?
God took such painstaking care
to provide the hare's slow and steady rival
with a custom made safe haven on his back,
and I wiped him out
in a wheel turn

Refiner of Silver

God sits as a refiner and purifier of silver,[59]
    and people.[60]
Wanting us to be the best we can be,
    He watches over us
as a silversmith carefully watches the
silver he places in the middle of the fire –
where the flames are the hottest,
to burn away all the impurities.

God, and the silversmith, keep their eyes on
the silver the entire time it is in the fire,
because they are aware
if they leave it too long in the flames
it will be destroyed.

I wondered how the silversmith can tell
when the process is complete.
I looked it up on the internet,
and the answer stunned me:
he knows the silver is fully refined
when he can see his image reflected in it.

---

[59] Malachi 3:3
[60] Psalm 66:10

Ghosts

I've never seen a ghost,
but I'm pretty sure my mother did
in the last months of her life.
We lived together, and it was unsettling
when she would talk about
the people riding in the back seat of our car,
the little children sitting at the kitchen table,
and the different dogs roaming through the house –
none of whom I could see.

I would have attributed her visions to
the side effects of medication, but we
had a little house dog who wasn't on any drugs,
and she seemed to see things too.
I would get goose bumps at night,
as I watched her sit up straight,
and follow with her eyes, someone or something,
moving around in our bedroom.

In retrospect, I wonder if mom was being given a
glimpse of a new life in heaven.
I could see God preparing her for the transition.
If that were the case, children being present
would make sense.
And though I didn't see the movie,
All Dogs Go To Heaven,
I am a dog lover, and tend to think
there may be some basis for that judgment.

In addition, Jesus told his disciples,
a ghost does not have flesh and bones as you see I have.[61]
He didn't say –
there is no such thing
as a ghost.

61 Luke 24:39

The Greatest of All Lighthouse Keepers

In the days when oil lamps and clockwork mechanisms
were used in the operation of lighthouses,
the lighthouse keeper was responsible for
    taking care of the lighthouse, its light and lens.
It was imperative he remained vigilant, stayed alert and on the job
no matter how bad the storm, or dire the circumstances.
The powerful beacon of light warned navigators of
dangerous rocks, or helped guide them into port –
showed them the way home.

In the book of Revelation the apostle John wrote,
there will be no need for the sun and moon in heaven
    as God and Jesus will be the lights.[62] I've read stories
about people who have had near-death experiences.
Many report having seen a bright light.
Kind of makes me wonder if
    there's a lighthouse on heaven's shore
tended by the greatest of all
lighthouse keepers.

---

[62] Revelation 21:23

Genocide

I received a letter from a friend telling me she had an M.E.
I didn't know what that meant, so I looked it up.
It stands for menstrual extraction, or abortion.
I remember feeling sick, and thinking:
in my mind, M. E. stands for
        the death of someone
                named ME.

I have a cousin who is a neurosurgeon, who was adopted at birth.
I imagine his patients, if they knew, would feel thankful
his birth mother chose adoption over abortion.
In the United States alone, since Roe vs. Wade in 1973
there have been somewhere in the neighborhood of
sixty million abortions – roughly ten times the number of people
        slaughtered in the Holocaust.

God told Jeremiah, before He formed him in the womb
He knew him,[63] and He knew the plans He had for him, plans to
prosper him, and not to harm him, plans to give him hope,
and a future.[64] I think we can assume God knows the plans
He has for us as well. Can you imagine being God, and knowing
who each of those babies would have been had they lived?

---

[63] Jeremiah 1:5
[64] Jeremiah 29:11

Music

Then I heard every creature in heaven and on earth
and under the earth and on the sea, and all that is in them, singing . . . [65]

Early in the morning
before the heat became oppressive,
I went outside to turn on the lawn sprinkler.
As the sun began to peek above the horizon
it sounded like every bird in the universe
was singing praises to God.
I listened a few minutes,
moved the sprinkler,
and went back in the house.

A short time later
I looked out the livingroom window,
and was surprised to see a raccoon
sitting beside the sprinkler.
The spray shot high in the air, arcing
from one side of the yard to the other.
The raccoon was moving his paws
through the strands of water
like a harpist plucking the strings of a harp.
I watched in amazement,
and wondered
if the angels could hear music.

---

[65]   Revelation 5:13

The Hummingbirds Will Return

Fifteen years ago I moved to the foothills of the Arkansas Ozarks.
Every year since then I have mixed sugar water, and filled
hummingbird feeders, which I like to watch out my kitchen window.
The tiny emerald gems bejeweled in ruby necklaces
arrive the first, or second, week of April. They never fail to
show up. I always look forward to seeing the first one
peek in the window, treading air.

These miraculous little birds stay about six months,
migrating by mid–October. I don't see them for the half–year
they are away, but based on what birding experts say,
I believe when they leave our area they fly hundreds of miles south –
crossing the Gulf of Mexico to winter in countries located
between southern Mexico, and northern Panama. Some even
hang out in the islands of the Caribbean.

Hold that picture –

Occasionally I read Oprah Winfrey's column in, *O Magazine*,
"What I know For Sure."
That title was the seed for this poem.
I can't see Jesus Christ sitting on his throne in heaven
anymore than I can see the hummingbirds in Central America.

But based on the Holy Bible, I believe Jesus is there,
seated at the right hand of God.[66]
Unlike the hummingbirds,
I don't know when He is coming back.
No one knows that, but God. [67]
What I know for sure is:
He will be back[68]
to take his people home –
just as I know
the hummingbirds will return
in the spring.

---

[66]   Ephesians 1:20
[67]   Matthew 24:36
[68]   I Thessalonians 4:16–17

Fruit Dove

Pastel colors of pink, green, yellow,
orange, and blue –
native to the countries of southeast Asia's rain forest,
including Cambodia –
killing fields of the
Khmer Rouge.

The male Pink-necked
Green Pigeon, or Fruit Dove,
is camouflaged amidst lush green leaves,
and colorful flowers –
more perfect and beautiful
than hand painted porcelain –
like a phoenix
risen from the ashes.

Opossums

One year my mother nearly died
with tick fever. She was left with residual
health problems the remainder of her life.
So when I learned that opossums
eat ticks,

I gained a new respect for them.
I used to think their beady eyes and bald tail
made them look like a giant rat. Then one day
I saw a mother opossum trudging
through the woods,

weighted down like a miner's pack mule,
with a passel of twelve large joeys
clinging
to her back and sides.

And I was reminded –
looks can never tell you
the strength
of someone's heart.

Old Barns and Old Folks

The year was 1972 when country singer, Tom T. Hall
hit number one on the Country Singles Chart
with a song he wrote called,
Old Dogs, Children and Watermelon Wine.

My racquetball brain bounced a connection
between that song, and this poem about old barns
and old folks. I get a nostalgic feeling when I see
old barns with a weathered look. I know they have
withstood years of rain, snow, ice, wind, and sun.
They may be faded, leaning a little, have a few
woodpecker holes, be charred from lightning –
have boards missing or be patched with tin,
but they're still standing.

It's kind of the same with old folks
who have lived through years of hard work,
seasons of sickness, and the death of loved ones.
Etched in their faces are strong character lines.
Their hair may be snow white,
and they may have skin cancers from hours
spent in the sun. They might soak their
teeth in a cup at night, have hearing aides,
eyeglasses, and walk with a cane,
but they haven't given up on life.

In His Word, God tells us we are to,
Stand up in the presence of the aged,
and show respect for the elderly...[69]
And as a dear friend recently
pointed out,
"It takes a lot of guts to grow old."

---

[69]   Leviticus 19:32

Princess

I was named after my maternal grandmother, who this book is dedicated to. She was a very humble person, and it seems to me she spent her life taking care of others. After her husband ran off, and her six living children were grown and gone from home, she worried about them, and her grandchildren – all the while continuing to look after the remnant of a menagerie of dogs, cats, pigs, chickens, a horse, and a cow. One dog I specifically remember had red mange and was bald over most of her body, with a few open sores and wispy patches of hair. Grandma treated the mange with used motor oil, and petted the dog with her hands. As you can imagine, the dog was a little on the ugly side, but in Grandma's eyes she was beautiful. She named her Princess, and lovingly cared for her until the day the good Lord called her home. It occurs to me, most people would not have touched that dog. In fact, many might have taken her out in the woods, and shot her.

Along a similar vein – most people in Jesus' time would not have wanted to be in close proximity to a leper, let alone touch one. But filled with compassion, Jesus reached out his hand and touched the leper.[70] He didn't have to do that. There are other scriptural examples of Him healing people by just speaking words. Wouldn't this world be a better place if each of us showed as much compassion?

---

[70] Mark 1:41

Peace Treaty

At the Native American Treaties Exhibit
in the Smithsonian's National Museum of the American Indian,
there is an exhibit of Broken Promises.
What a sad commentary.

Unlike people who sometimes speak with forked tongues,
and the devil who is the father of lies,
God keeps His promises.[71]
Scripture tells us, it is impossible for Him to lie.[72]

When I look at the cross, at the vertical timber
that points from earth to heaven,
I am excited to think of the journey I will one day take.
And the horizontal timber reminds me
of the welcoming arms of God.

Since God is Holy, and can't live in the presence of evil,
He devised a plan to be reconciled with the creation He loves.
To me the cross is a symbol of that plan – a peace treaty between
God and man, signed by God in His own blood. And He gives us
free choice - to accept, or decline, the terms of the treaty
outlined in His Word.

---

71 Joshua 23:14
72 Hebrews 6:18

Beavers

The only time I remember being lost in the woods
was on a cloudy afternoon in Michigan when I stumbled upon
a beaver pond. Taking photos as I made my way around the pond
and watched the beavers work, I didn't pay attention
to where I started from, and the water meandered over a large area.

I saw one beaver gnaw a small tree down,
then float it up a canal to the lodge. Another one
was eating the bark off a branch he held in his paws,
rotating it the way we eat corn-on-the-cob.

When a coyote came for a drink, the beaver nearest me
smacked his tail hard on the water, and all beavers
dove under – like in those submarine movies
where someone yells, "dive, dive!"

By that time I realized it was getting late, and I had no idea
how to get back to camp. I continued to walk, and eventually
came upon a hunting party. The men there were nice enough
to transport me in the back of their pick-up. Once on pavement,
I was able to give them directions through the sliding rear window.

The next day I returned home,
and did a little reading about nature's engineers.
I'd like to share three nuggets:
a beavers' teeth never stop growing,
so they can chew on hardwoods their entire lives;
they were created with special oil glands
that allow them to waterproof their fur;
and my favorite – they have a
second set of eyelids that are clear
like designer swim goggles.

We're All in This Together

The cows needed to be fed.
The seventy-seven year old man moved a little slower
than he used to. He reached for his jacket
hanging by the door. His arthritic fingers fumbled
as he buttoned it. When he was younger
he wouldn't have worn the jacket, but these days
the biting cold seemed to seep into his bones.
He opened the door, and bowed his head
into the wind.

Chickens pecked at the ground
as he crossed the barn yard.
A tiny bird sat on the edge of the water trough.
It didn't move as he approached.
When he got closer he could see
the bird's feet were frozen to the trough.
He cupped his large, leathered hands
around the bird, and stood there a few minutes.
The ice thawed. He opened his hands,
and the bird flew.

Pride

Ten of us who were together on a backpack trip in Arizona came to a long, cold, deep, pool of water amid boulders. We had to cross it to get to our destination on time. One of the two student instructors asked if there was anyone who couldn't swim well, as they had brought inner tubes to float our packs, that we could hold onto. Another girl, and I, acknowledged we weren't good swimmers, and agreed to accompany the tubes. The instructors, and some of the others, swam to the opposite side. I was kicking my way across when about midway, I spotted a stocky, six foot two-inch New Yorker going under. He went down and came back up three times. When I realized he was in trouble, I yelled for help. The only ones close enough to him were the two of us hanging onto the tubes, and two teenage girls. One of them, petite, wouldn't go near the guy for fear he would drown her. The other girl was six foot tall, seventeen years old, and was trained in life-saving. She dove down, came up from behind, grabbed him around his chest, and swam to shore with him in tow. The guy was wiped out, and the rest of us were so upset that we made camp right there at mid-day. In His Word God tells us, *pride goes before destruction, a haughty spirit before a fall.*[73] A strapping twenty-one year old with his priceless life ahead of him came close to dying that day because he was too proud to admit he wasn't a strong swimmer.

---

[73] Proverbs 16:18

Reincarnation

I am one hundred percent positive I never lived a previous life
because God tells us in His Word man is destined to die once,
and after that to face judgment.[74] He also reminds us,
our lives on earth are brief – we are a mist,[75]
a passing breeze,[76] a flower of the field. [77]

That being said –
if I had lived another life before this one,
I am relatively certain I would have been a hobo
riding the rails. For many of the Halloweens of my childhood
that was the costume I chose to wear. Yes ladies, I know I am
a female. But like Sgt. Joe Friday in the fifties television show,
Dragnet, "I'm just, stating the facts, ma'am."

In my mid-teens, I dragged my two little cousins,
the brothers I never had, along with me as we hiked
the thirty-five acres owned by our aunt and uncle.
Railroad tracks ran along the back of the property,
and we walked the tracks to a trestle above a creek,
where we would sit and dangle our feet
as we watched the resident muskrat swim.

My dad was career military, and we moved quite a bit
when I was growing up. He always tried to get rid of
as many nonessential items as possible before the movers came.
The only thing of mine I recall begging him not to give away
was a train set I got for Christmas when I was seven.

---

[74] Hebrews 9:27
[75] James 4:14
[76] Psalm 78:39
[77] Pslm103:15-16

Bless his softy heart he didn't, and I still have it to this day.

Awhile back at a craft fair I came upon a wooden carving of a hobo
with a Benji-faced dog poking out of the bindle, or blanket stick,
he was carrying. Of course, I bought it. It hangs
on my bedroom wall, and brings a smile to my hobo heart.

Polar Bears

The Norse poets of medieval Scandinavia called the polar bear, *Rider of Icebergs, White Sea Deer, Whale's Bane, Sailor of the Floe, and Seal's Dread.* Polar bears have been spotted swimming one hundred miles from land, and are known to regularly swim distances of thirty miles at speeds up to six miles per hour. They feed mainly on the fat rich skin and blubber of seals, walruses, and beluga whales. And according to the people who know such things, polar bears aren't really white. Clear guard hairs and sunlight have something to do with them appearing to be. Able to stay warm in freezing arctic temperatures, and ice cold water, their outer guard hairs are hollow tubes that fill with air, and hold in body heat. Beneath that they have a dense, thick undercoat of fur. Below that their skin is black, which is thought to maximize the absorption of solar radiation. And underneath their skin is a two to four inch-thick layer of fat, or blubber. Isn't God a phenomenal Creator?

Monarch Butterflies

As daylight hours shorten,
   nights become cooler,
      and milkweed plants turn yellow,
         dehydrate, and become covered with

sooty mold from aphids.
   And sun-related directional sensors,
      located in the antennae of monarch
         butterflies, will guide millions of

them, thousands of miles south
   to the Oyamel fir forest
      in central Mexico. There they will hibernate,
         draped in massive cape-like bunches of

orange, black, and white –
   if vampire bats,
      Hitchcock would have loved
         that frightening sight.

Vultures

Sign of death –
dark circling carnivores -
hated scavengers soaring in their wide wingspans.
Up-close ugly, bald heads and necks,
sharp-hooked beaks ripping, tearing
chunks of rotting infected carrion.
Gorging until unable to fly,
then regurgitating to lighten the load
and get airborne.

Jesus said, *wherever there is a carcass,*
there the vultures will gather.[78]

Vultures have been endowed with a strong
immune system that allows them to eat
rotting and infected meat without becoming ill.
In addition, their bald head and neck
lowers their risk of contracting diseases
since bacteria can become lodged in feathers.
Vultures can also projectile vomit ten feet
as a defense against predators.

Imagine the increase of human maladies
if the world was without vultures –
to clean up dead, rotting, infected animals, birds, fish,
and reptiles. I hope the next time I see them circling in the sky,
or in a disheveled huddle on the road,
I think about that, and
thank God for creating them.

---

[78] Matthew 24:28

Raccoons

Three a.m., dark as a dungeon,
I hear sounds at the window.
I drag myself out of bed,
and stumble through the dining room
to flip on the outside light.

Quickly I raise the blinds,
and am face to face with
two raccoons. The young one drops
from the hummingbird feeder,
and skedaddles across the yard.

The old, fat one
lumbers down, and away from
the seed feeder that hangs from the eave.
Bandits, burglars,
robbers, thieves –
no wonder God gave them masks.

Heartsick

I spent ten years of my working life doing social work. A few times I had to visit people in prisons. I hated the loud clanking sound the steel doors made when they closed and locked behind me on my way to the visitation window. There was a finality about the sound, and I would get a sick feeling in the pit of my stomach. Before God opened the floodgates of heaven to destroy every living thing,[79] except righteous Noah, his family, and the animals and birds He sent to be saved along with them – when they were all safely tucked inside – God shut the door to the ark.[80] Evidently, since the earth was corrupt and full of violence,[81] He felt the need to start things over. I can't help but believe though, He had to be heartsick when he closed that door knowing every living thing outside the ark was about to perish. [82]

---

[79] Genesis 7:11
[80] Genesis 7:16
[81] Genesis 6:11
[82] Genesis 7:21

Optical Illusions

Years ago in Michigan
I read a newspaper article about mushroom hunters
who died after eating false morels. One day last week
I went outside to feed my cat, and spotted a large walking stick
on the tan brick of the house. It had been years
since I'd seen one of those, and I marveled at
how much it really did look like a stick with legs.
Another time I saw a leafy green walking leaf
walking – what a strange sight! Recently I watched
a video of what looked like an orchid flower –
until it started crawling around on a person's hand.
Pink and white with lobes on its legs, it was an orchid mantis,
native to Malaysia, and southeast Asia's rain forest.

I live in Arkansas. We have six species of venomous snakes.
We also have thirty species of non-poisonous snakes.
Two of them - the scarlet, and the milk snake,
are similar in appearance to the Texas coral snake
whose neurotoxic venom can cause extreme pain, or even death.
What is the message?
Maybe God in His brilliance
tries to warn us,
to show us by example -
we need to be careful, slow down, pay attention,
because things are not always
what they seem.

Kangaroo Brief

Bounce . . . bounce . . . bounce . . .
kickbox!
Hop . . . hop . . . hop . . .
kickbox!
Jump . . . jump . . . jump . . .
kickbox!
Leap . . . leap . . . leap . . .
kickbox!
Spring . . . spring . . . spring . . .
kickbox!
Silly people,
do you really think
you
invented kickboxing?

Eagle and the Snake

I recall from childhood,
grown-ups talking about a story in the newspaper.
At a local swimming hole
where people jumped from a rock cliff into a river,
a man saw a water moccasin gliding through the water
towards a child. He swam between the snake and the child,
and the snake attacked him. Before rescuers
could get him out of the water,
the snake bit the man eleven times.
He didn't survive.

Recently I watched a video of an eagle
battling a large rattlesnake. The eagle didn't attempt
to fight the snake on the ground, the snake's territory.
Swooping from the sky,
the eagle snatched the snake with its talons,
and flew a good distance
before dropping it to its death on rocks.
The video contained an underlying message:

to be victorious like the eagle,
who feasted upon his deadly adversary,
we shouldn't try to fight the devil,
the evil serpent, on his turf. We need to
study the Word of God, and pray -
lift our battles into spiritual realms,
place them in God's hands.

Emperor Penguins

In the extreme harshness of an Antarctic winter,
when winds sometimes howl at speeds of nearly
two hundred miles per hour, and temperatures can plummet
to around minus one hundred and thirty-five degrees Fahrenheit,
female emperor penguins each lay one egg.

The father penguins pluck out feathers
under a flap of belly skin, and use their beaks
to nudge their egg on top of their feet, wriggling
until it is safely tucked away next to the brood patch.
For two months the fathers stay huddled together
against the bitter cold – barely moving, and eating nothing.

Meanwhile, the females journey to the ocean to feed,
and store up fat before they return to care for the young chicks.
Born naked, the chicks snuggle under
the fathers built-in shelter, and are kept warm
by his body heat. I wonder if there could be
a more tender example
of how nature mirrors providence,
the protective care of God?

Zebra

Horse tiger –
　　wild, untamable,
　　　　no saddle sits your back.
　　　　　　Who endowed you with wisdom
　　　　　　　　to follow the rains –
　　　　　　　　　　the grasses, the leaves?

　　　　　　The documentary special
　　　　　showed thousands of you migrating
　　　　hundreds of miles on the Serengeti –
　　each unique in your
prison clothes design.

Zebra free,
　　running for your life,
　　　　whinny if you will –
　　　　　　are you white with black stripes,
　　　　　　　　or black with white?

Garments of Skin

In the garden of Eden
when Adam and Eve disobeyed God,
sin and death entered the world.
God, disappointed at their behavior,
assigned consequences –
Eve's pains in childbearing would be greatly increased;
Adam would painfully toil the ground all the days of his life.[83]
Notice though, God didn't withhold His love.
Scripture tells us, He made garments of skin,
and clothed Adam and Eve.[84]

And in the New Testament,
when the teachers of the law and the Pharisees
brought in a woman caught in adultery,
and made her stand before a group of people –
Jesus could have gone along with them
when they said, in the law Moses commanded that they
stone such women.[85] And He could have called the woman
belittling names, but that isn't how God operates. Rather,
He told the people if any of them were
without sin, they should be the first
to throw a stone at her.[86]

---

83   Genesis 3:16–17
84   Genesis 3:21
85   John 8:3–5
86   John 8:7

A Line in the Sand

The aerial photograph of the Gulf of Alaska
is striking. It looks like two distinct oceans meet
at an invisible boundary line, and don't merge.
The water on the left is a light turquoise –
on the right an indigo blue.

Experts report that the lighter color is
glacial melt water from the coast of Alaska,
and the darker indigo is general ocean water.
Supposedly the color variation has to do with
differences in temperature, density, sediments,
and salinity levels.

While all that may be true,
I propose the possibility of a more biblical explanation –
that for a providential reason unknown to man,[87]
God drew a line in the sand *which we can't see,*
and commanded each of the bodies of water
not to cross it.[88]

---

[87] Isaiah 55:8–9
[88] Isaiah 55:8–9, Psalm 104:5–9, Job 38:8–11

Giraffe

Tall and gentle sentinel,
   rarely napping
      watchtower of the African plains –
        a living patchwork quilt,
          a walking jigsaw puzzle,
            a breathing, stained glass pattern on stilts.
          Can you see God smiling
            as he meted the giraffe's neck,
           and molded his sweet,
                sweet face?

Missing Hearts

Is there anything that ignites the fires of righteous anger faster
than injustices that involve children? In a perfect world,
we believe, children should be able to grow up
skipping and giggling with dancing eyes,
tearing the wrapping paper off of life –
exempt from the ravages of child predators.

But for decades the faces of missing children have haunted
milk cartons, grocery sacks, cereal boxes, billboards, IRS booklets, posters,
direct mail flyers, television newscasts, the world wide web,
and electronic highway signs. I won't name names,
though I remember the names of some of the children –
like the six year-old boy in Florida kidnapped from the
toy section of a department store, and decapitated.

Only God knows why such things happen.

On second thought, that's not true.
Such things happen because evil exists. But we can thank God
there is coming a day when it won't.[89]
In the meantime,

---

[89] I Corinthians 15: 24-26

I try to imagine the heartache, and emotional pain
of a parent whose child is missing. I can't.
The best I can do is recall a young actress
on a television talk show who spoke about
her first baby – a daughter, who had recently learned to walk.
She said, *I feel like my heart has grown legs,*
and is walking around outside my body.
I suspect, anyone whose child is missing,
feels as if their heart is too.

Marine Iguanas

Snorkeling on a guided tour of the Galapagos Islands, I did a double-take when I saw my first live marine iguana swimming underwater. Four to five feet long, it looked like a throwback to the dinosaurs – with a fierce look, spiky dorsal scales, and a knotty head. When I saw a second iguana with long sharp claws clinging to a large rock, its crocodile like tail swaying in the current, I would have gotten out of the water immediately if the guide hadn't previously explained that iguanas are gentle herbivores that feed on algae and seaweed. He also informed us: the Galapagos archipelago is the only known place on earth where marine iguanas are found; there are many sizes, shapes, and colors of them, and they have razor-sharp teeth that enable them to scrape algae off rocks. Back at the hotel I did an internet search, and learned: iguanas were created with glands that clean their blood of the extra salt they ingest while feeding. The glands are located near their nose, and they sneeze frequently to blow the salt out. The salt often lands on their head, which becomes encrusted, giving them their unique knotty looks. Don't you find this world the most curious place?

The Promised Land

A land that stretches afar,[90]
a land of broad rivers and streams,[91]
  a new heaven, a new earth,[92]
   the home of righteousness.[93]
A place unlike anything
 we have ever imagined.[94]
People from every nation,
tribe, and language;[95]
everlasting joy,[96]
and ten thousand times ten thousand
    angels singing.[97]
No death, mourning, crying, or pain.[98]
The leopard will lie down with the goat,
  the wolf will live with the lamb,
the cow will feed with the bear,
  the lion will eat straw like the ox,[99]
 and no one
will harm or destroy.[100]

---

[90] Isaiah 33:17
[91] Isaiah 33:21
[92] Revelation 21:1
[93] 2 Peter 3:13
[94] I Corinthians 2:9
[95] Revelation 7:9
[96] Isaiah 35:10
[97] Revelation 5:11–12
[98] Revelation 21:4
[99] Isaiah 11:6–7
[100] Isaiah 11:9

Volcano

I recall being captivated by the flow of molten lava in 1961
when I watched the movie, *The Devil At Four O' Clock,*
starring Spencer Tracy and Frank Sinatra. It told the story
of a volcano erupting, and children being rescued
from a mountain health clinic.

My fascination with lava was fanned into flames over the years
by television newscasts that showed rivers of glowing
orange-yellow lava flowing down mountainsides.
Recently my curiosity was stoked by an internet video
of Hawaii Volcanoes National Park,
and a lava waterfall streaming over a cliff
into the ocean.

A little research, and my lay interpretation of a volcano is:
it's a vent that allows the pressure of hot gases, ash,
and molten rock to escape from deep inside the earth.
At the surface they are liquefied at extreme temperatures.
I admit, I am in awe of God's genius. And now
I would like to ask you a question –
if there were no volcanoes,
do you think the earth might explode?

Patting Down the Dirt

Moses, servant of the Lord,[101]
the most humble man
on the face of the earth, [102]
and the only person mentioned in the Bible
to have been buried by God.[103]
In my mind's eye
I see God kneeling –
a teardrop sliding
from his cheek to the ground,
His hands gently patting down the dirt
atop Moses' grave

---

[101] Joshua 1:1
[102] Numbers 12:3
[103] Deuteronomy 34:5-6

Illegal Drugs

The eight month old baby
weighed eight pounds.
The Children's Hospital doctor said,
another twenty-four hours,
and he would have been dead.
The baby's parents were furious
with Children's Protective Services
for removing him from the home.
Cocaine addicts, they insisted
there was nothing wrong with him.

Illegal drug usage is one of the scourges
of our generation. God created people
to be in a close relationship with Him.
Those who haven't cultivated that relationship,
may feel as though there is a gaping hole inside them,
and try to fill it with anything they can –
illegal drugs, alcohol, pornography,
gambling, a long list.

Meth was involved another time
when I had to drive to an elementary school
to transport a seven year-old girl,
and her six year-old brother,
for placement in foster care.
On the way to the home
I explained to the kids that their mom
had been arrested, was in jail,
and didn't have the money to bond out.

After a minute of silence,
from the back seat I heard
the little girl's hopeful voice say,
"I could pick up pretty rocks
and sell them to make money,
so mommy could get out of jail."

Porcupines

A lady walking towards me in Walmart the other day
had on a T-shirt that read, *Free Hugs* –
with a photo of a porcupine in full bloom
defense mode.
I like that.

Reminded me of the time our golden retriever,
and the neighbor's black lab,
returned from a romp in the woods
with their slobbery tongues hanging out,
and their laughing faces peppered
with needle-like quills.

God made sure the rotund, slow-moving quill pigs
have a way to protect themselves
as they mosey along,
minding their own business,
munching leaves.

Panoramic Canvas

Sky of white ripples, clouds
unlike any I have ever seen –
      altocumulus, mackerel, buttermilk.
What a blessing to be able to see the sky,
day or night, free of charge.
Like paintings on a panoramic canvas
      in constant motion –
pink, orange, yellow sunrise;
white, gray, black, feathery,
billowing, lightning-streaked clouds;
   rainbow;
      hawk soaring;
geese in formation;
      snowflakes drifting;
orange, red, sun ball descending,
moon rising, silver stars.
From my frame of mind
all we have to do is look up
to see a view lovelier
than the ceiling of the Sistine Chapel.

Stradivarius

What comes to mind when you hear
the name Stradivarius? I envision
the most expensive, highest quality violin.
A little research reveals there is more.
Antonio Stradivari was an Italian luthier,
maker of stringed instruments –
violins, cellos, violas, guitars and harps.
He lived during the seventeenth and
eighteenth centuries, and was considered
the greatest artisan in the field.

A Stradivarius is one of the stringed instruments
crafted by him, or one of his family members,
and the name implies excellence in sound quality.
By association, being called the Stradivari in any field
is to be considered the finest there is.

And if you think about it, the high value
placed on a Stradivarius is based on
the reputation of the one who made it.
Let that sink in. Then think about
mankind. We were made by the God
who created the universe, and
everything in it.[104] Not only that,
He made us in His own image.[105]

---

[104] John 1:3
[105] Genesis 1:27

So we are kind of like a Stradivarius, only better.
And as a Stradivarius adds beauty to the world
by the lovely music it produces,
our Maker expects us to do the same,[106]
and bring glory to His name.

---

[106] Ephesians 2:10

Fear of the Lord

Solomon said, the fear of the Lord is the beginning of wisdom.[107]
He also said, to fear the Lord is to hate evil.[108]
My brain makes a connection –
hating evil is the beginning of wisdom.
That makes me think there may be hope for me
as I have no trouble hating evil.

My childhood was spent in the fifties
watching television shows like Lassie, Leave It To Beaver,
Roy Rogers, The Mickey Mouse Club, Rin Tin Tin,
and I Love Lucy. It seems to me
those shows were indicative of life at that time –
moms often stayed at home,
dads tried to give their kids guidance,
heroes came to the rescue, and comedians were funny
without being obscene.

I was a Brownie scout,
and went throughout the neighborhood
selling Girl Scout cookies for fifty cents a box.
At Halloween, we kids trick-or-treated door to door
while our moms or dads waited on the sidewalk.

My best friend had a Radio Flyer red wagon,
and we would scavenge areas not far from home
collecting soda bottles which we cashed in at
a nearby mom and pop grocery for two cents each.

---

[107] Proverbs 9:10
[108] Proverbs 8:13

We thought we were rich as we bought wax coke bottles
filled with syrup, wax lips and moustaches, Lik–M–Aid
packets, and an assortment of penny candies and gum.
I was seven, and my friend was five. I don't recall
ever hearing anyone talk about child abductions,
sexual predators, or serial murderers.

Television shows often taught family values. Curse words
were seldom used. Private matters weren't openly
discussed – people blushed if someone did,
and violence wasn't in your face, bloody, gross graphic.

I don't know where it all went south,
but I feel like we adults owe today's children an apology.
It could be, as Edmund Burke said,
"the only thing necessary for the triumph of evil
is for good men to do nothing."
Or as David of the Holy Bible wrote,
the wicked freely strut about
when what is vile is honored among men.[109]

---
[109] Psalm 12:8

Owls

One of my least favorite sounds
is the panicked screams
of a rabbit in the middle of the night
when an owl sinks his talons in the rabbit's back,
lifts him high in the air,
and answers his own question,
"who–who–who, who–who–who?"

Gifted by God with excellent hearing, as well as
day and night vision, and the ability to turn their heads
two hundred and seventy degrees, owls rarely miss their prey.
I watched a television newscast showing Florida fruit growers
who placed owl nesting boxes throughout their groves
to help curb the mice problem.

And one day in winter I saw a white owl sitting on
the black bone of a limb. He had little gray
heart-shaped markings on his chest and belly. I'm not lying.

I was reminded of Pulitzer Prize winning poet,
Mary Oliver's poem, *The Kingfisher,*
in which she wrote, "I think this is the prettiest world –
so long as you don't mind a little dying."

Valley of the Shadow of Death

I used to think the valley of the shadow of death[110] was a place
we have to walk through
at the end of our lives. The other day
I took a trip down memory lane
as I looked at the photos that line the hallway
in our home. I remembered good times
with friends and family who are long gone now,
and it dawned on me:
we live in the valley of the shadow of death
our entire lives,
and everyone dies –
no exceptions.

The best part is, death is not the end,
but a glorious new beginning.
And what is the likelihood,
the same God who has taken such wonderful care of us
throughout our lives on earth,
will be right there to give us a hand up
as we transition out of this
sometimes dark valley
into the brightest light we have ever known?

---

[110] Psalm 23:4

AFTERWORD

I would like to thank you, the reader, for investing your time – a cantle of your crazy, beautiful life – in reading this book. I would also mention that I pray for wisdom, and the guidance of the Holy Spirit, when I write. I never know what God is going to place on my heart. Not in a million years would it have occurred to me, I would one day write about vultures. That was kind of a T. M. I. (too much information) kind of experience, even for me. I wrote this collection of poems, as well as the first collection, *The Magnanimous Gift,* as presents for God. But isn't it just like Him – I am the one who received the blessing.

ACKNOWLEDGEMENTS

Special thanks to:

- Poet, Mary Oliver, A Poetry Handbook: A Prose Guide To Understanding And Writing Poetry, copyright 1994.
- Author, Dinty W. Moore, The Mindful Writer: Noble Truths of the Writing Life, copyright 2012.
- Faithwriters.com, where an earlier version of a few poems previously appeared.
- Writer's Digest Books, and the following magazines:
- Writer's Digest
- The Writer
- Poets & Writers

Printed in the United States
By Bookmasters